Shakespeare's Christmas Gift To Queen Bess

In the year 1596

By

Anna Benneson McMahan

[ZHINGOORA BOOKS]

This edition is published by
Zhingoora Books.

The Cover is Designed by Pallav Sethiya.

CONTENTS

I.

At the Mermaid.

Thus Raleigh, thus immortal Sidney shone

(Illustrious names!) in great Eliza's days.

--Thos. Edwardes.

At the Mermaid

The numberless diamond-shaped window panes of the Mermaid Tavern are twinkling like so many stars in the chill December air of London. It is the last meeting of the Mermaid Club for the year

1596, and not a member is absent. As they drop in by twos and threes and gather in groups about the room, it is plain that expectation is on tip-toe. They call each other by their Christian names and pledge healths. Some are young, handsome, fastidious in person and dress; others are bohemian in costume, speech, and action; all wear knee breeches, and nearly all have pointed beards. He of the harsh fighting face, of the fine eye and coarse lip and the shaggy hair, whom they call Ben, although one of the youngest is yet plainly one of the leaders both for wit and for wisdom.

The River Avon at Stratford

"I know a bank where the wild thyme blows,

Where oxlips and the nodding violet grows."

That grave and handsome gentleman whose lordly bearing and princely dress mark his high rank, is another favourite. He has written charming poems, has fought gallantly on many fields, has voyaged widely on many seas, has founded colonies in distant America, is a favourite of the Queen. But in this Mermaid Club his chief glory is that he is its founder and leader, the one whose magnetism and personal charm has summoned and cemented in friendship all these varied elements.

At last the all-important matter of the yearly Christmas play at court has been settled; the Master of the Revels has chosen from the rich stores of his manuscripts "_The Midsummer Night's Dream_", graciously adding that "for wit and mirth it is like to please her Majesty exceedingly." A high honor, indeed, for its author. For, not then, as now, were plays written primarily for the recreation and approval of the audience of the theatre. True, the public stage was fostered, and attracted its daily audience, but rather as a dress rehearsal, its main purpose being to train the players for the court presentations at one of her Majesty's palaces. The secret spur to both players and playwright was the hope of being among the chosen for the festivities at Richmond, Whitehall, or Greenwich, as the Queen might fancy to hold her court.

Birthplace of Mary Arden, Mother of Shakespeare

"Quite over-canopied with luscious woodbine

With sweet musk-roses and with eglantine."

Warwickshire House of the Tudor Period

Disappointment, soreness, jealousy, not seldom followed the award of the coveted distinction, but not so on this occasion. For now the successful candidate is one of the youngest and best beloved of this jolly coterie, and their pride in him is shown by the eagerness with which they await his coming to read to them the changes in the manuscript of his play since its former presentation. Ah! hear the burst of applause that greets his late arrival--a high-browed, sandy-haired man of thirty-two, lithe in figure, of middle height, with a smile of great sweetness, yet sad withal. On his face, one may read the lines of recent sorrow, and all know that he has returned but recently to London from the mournful errand which took him to his Stratford home--the burial of his dearly beloved and only son, Hamnet. The plaudits for the author of the most successful play of the season--"_Romeo and Juliet_," which was then taking the town by storm at the Curtain Theatre--were little heeded by the grief-stricken father as he urged his horse over the rough roads of the four days' journey, arriving just too late for a parting word from dying lips. But private sorrows are not for those who are called to public duties; a writer must trim his pen not to his own mood, but to the mood of the hour. And Queen Elizabeth, old in years, but ever young in her love of fun and frolic and flattery, must be made to forget the heaviness of time and the infirmities of age. If she may no longer take part in out-door sports--the hunting, the hawking, the bear-baiting,--she still may command processions, fêtes, masques, and stage-plays. It pleases her now to see this wonderful fairy piece, of which she has heard so much since, two years ago, it graced the nuptials of the Earl of Derby. Does she not remember also that pretty impromptu verse of the author when acting the part of King in another man's play, two years ago at Greenwich? Did she not twice drop her glove near his feet in crossing the stage? And how happily had he responded to the challenge! True to the character as well as to the metre of his part, he had picked up the glove, presenting it to its owner with the words:--

"And though now bent on this high embassy,

Yet stoop we to take up our cousin's glove."

Old Graves in Trinity Churchyard, Stratford

Seats are taken, the manuscript is opened, and the club becomes a green-room conference. The play is not to be recast entirely, the changes from the early version being mainly to introduce certain touches to flatter the royal ears, and to suit it to the more elaborate equipment of the Whitehall stage. Quill in hand, the reader as he proceeds crosses out from his manuscript everything that clogs the movement or detracts from the playfulness; giving free rein to his luxuriant imagination, he scatters the choicest flowers of fancy to create a vivid and animated picture. The lovers meet and part with pretty rhymes and repartee; the hard-handed men--the tradesmen and tinkers--bring their clumsy efforts to serve the wedding-feast; the fairies, graceful, lovely, enchanting, dance amidst the fragrance of enameled meadows.

Old Warwickshire Cottages

"And all things shall be peace."

His fellow writers feel the charm. No one of them can do work in so many kinds nor of such kind in each. They recognise their master, they are under his magic spell; the familiar stories from Plutarch and Chaucer and Ovid take on a new meaning; the very holly on the walls seems alive with the fairy folk, as indeed it should be, according to the pretty, old superstition that elves and fairies hover about all Christmas fêtes. Hence, branches are hanging in hall and bower in order that these invisible guests may "hang in each leaf and cling on every bough." The holly, its prickly leaves symbolic of the crown of thorns, and its red berries of the blood of Christ, banishes the ivy and other greens, and becomes the popular favourite that it has since remained, for Christmas decoration.

A Group of Morris Dancers

"The quaint-mazes in the wanton green,

For lack of tread, are undistinguishable."

A responsive audience truly. Roars of laughter greet the rollicking humour of the clowns and their rude burlesque of things theatrical. But longest and loudest is the applause over the new touches--those portions that have been written in to please the court and the Queen. To remodel a play written for a marriage celebration so that it shall seem to praise the virginity of the Queen were surely no slight task, but it has been accomplished.

Though the scene is laid in Greece, yet the play is full of the English life that all know so well. "Merrie England" and not classic Greece has given the poet the picture of the sweet country school-girls working at one flower, warbling one song, growing together like a double cherry. Of England, is the picture of the hounds with "ears that sweep away the morning dew"; from England, all this out-door woodland life, the clown's play and the clowns themselves,--Bottom with his inimitable conceit, and his fellows, Snug, Quince, and the rest. English is all Puck's fairy lore, the cowslips tall, the red-hipt humble-bee, Oberon's bank, the pansy love-in-idleness, and all the lovely imagery of the verse. English is the whole scenic background, and the "Wood near Athens" is plainly the Stratford boy's idealised memory of the Weir Brake that he knows so well.

Mayhap, in very truth, on some mid-summer night the young poet, even then of "imagination all compact," did indeed dream a dream or see a vision like unto this, bringing it from Stratford to London partly written, but foregoing its completion for labour that would find readier acceptance at the theatre.

Garden View of Shakespeare's Birthplace, Stratford

"An odorous chaplet of sweet summer buds."

However that may be, certain it is that this is a red-letter night at the Mermaid. The genius of "gentle Will" has taken a new point of departure and shines as it has not shone before either in his making over of other men's plays, or in his few original works. He has conquered a new realm of art; the phantoms of the fairy world for the first time have been endowed with a genuine and sustained dramatic interest. Small wonder that no one ventures to interrupt as the pages are turned; even at the close, only one, the Silenus-faced Ben, offers a criticism. Being well versed in classic lore, he protests against the characterisation of Theseus, Duke of Athens, saying it is too modern, and has in fact nothing of the antique or Grecian in its composition.

But he is over-ruled speedily, and as the meeting breaks up one of the younger fellows whispers to another, "Shakespeare was sent us from Heaven, but Jonson from--College."

II.

At the Queen's Palace.

Those flights upon the banks of Thames

That so did take Eliza and our James.

--Ben Jonson.

Queen Elizabeth going to Whitehall by the Thames

"But, noble Thames, whilst I can hold a pen,

I will divulge thy glory unto men."

John Taylor, the "Water Poet."

It is Christmas night. Lords, ladies, and ambassadors have been summoned to Whitehall Palace to witness the play for which author, actors, and artists of many kinds have been working so industriously during the past few weeks. The Banqueting Hall, with a temporary stage at one end, has been converted into a fine auditorium.

Facing the stage, and beneath her canopy of state, sits Queen Elizabeth, in ruff and farthingale, her hair loaded with crowns and powdered with diamonds, while her sharp smile and keen glance take note of every incident. Nearest her person and evidently the chief favourite of the moment, is the man who has long been considered the Adonis of the Court. He is now also its hero, having but recently returned from the wars in Spain, where his gallantry and promptitude at Cadiz have won new glories for Her Majesty. In five short years more, his head will come to the block by decree of this same Majesty; but this no one can foresee and all voices now unite in praises for the brave and generous Essex.

Earl of Essex

Another conspicuous favourite is a blue-eyed, pink-cheeked young fellow of twenty-three, whose scarcely perceptible beard and moustache, and curly auburn hair falling over his shoulders and half-way to his waist, would suggest femininity except for his martial manner and tall figure. His resplendent attire is notable even in this gorgeously arrayed company. His white satin doublet has a broad collar, edged with lace and embroidered with silver thread; the white trunks and knee-breeches are laced with gold; the sword-belt, embroidered in red and gold, is decorated at intervals with white silk bows; purple garters, embroidered in silver thread, fasten the white stockings below the knee. As one of the handsomest of Elizabeth's courtiers, and also one of the most distinguished for birth, wealth, and wit, he would be a striking figure at any time; but to-night he has the added distinction of being the special friend and munificent patron of the author of the play that they have come to witness. To him had been dedicated the author's first appeal to the reading public--a poem called "Venus and Adonis," published some three years since; also, a certain "sugared sonnet," privately circulated, protesting--

"For to no other pass my verses tend

Than of your graces and your gifts to tell."

And through the patronage of this man--the gracious Earl of Southampton--the actor-author was first brought to the Queen's notice, finally leading to the present distinction at her hands.

Earl of Southampton

But now the stage compels attention. The silk curtains are withdrawn, disclosing a setting of such elaboration and illusion as never before has been witnessed by sixteenth century eyes.

Never before has the frugal Elizabeth consented to such an expenditure for costumes, properties, lights, and music. In vain the audience awaits the coming of the author; he is behind the scenes, an anxious and watchful partner with the machinist in securing the proper working of these new mechanical appliances, and the smoothness of the scene shifting. The Queen is a connoisseur in these matters, and there must be no bungling.

The stage is divided horizontally between the roof and floor, the upper part concealed from the audience, while the lower section represents the interior of a royal palace at Athens. Three soundings of the cornet announce the opening of the play with its stately dialogue, in which Theseus, Duke of Athens, and Hippolyta, Queen of the Amazons, anticipate their approaching nuptials. Egeus enters with his daughter Hermia to bring complaint to the Duke that she will not marry Demetrius, the husband he has selected for her, but is bewitched with love for Lysander. The Duke reasons with Hermia; but the maiden is still obdurate and demands to know the worst that may befall if she refuses to wed Demetrius. The Duke pronounces sentence:--

"Either to die the death, or to abjure

Forever the society of men.

Therefore, fair Hermia, question your desires.

Know of your youth, examine well your blood,

Whether, if you yield not to your father's choice,

You can endure the livery of a nun,

For aye to be in shady cloister mew'd,

To live a barren sister all your life,

Chanting faint hymns to the cold, fruitless moon,

Thrice blessed they that master so their blood,

To undergo such maiden pilgrimage;

But earthlier happy is the rose distill'd

Than that which withering on the virgin thorn

Grows, lives, and dies in single blessedness."

Queen Elizabeth listening to the Play

The tributes to the "maiden pilgrimage" and "single blessedness" win from the Queen's countenance a glow which age has had no power to diminish. The highway to favour with the Virgin Queen, as every courtier and every writer knows, lies through praises of her voluntary state of celibacy.

Thus threatened, Hermia is urged by Lysander to a clandestine marriage:--

"If thou lov'st me then,

Steal forth thy father's house to-morrow night,

And in the wood, a league without the town,

Where I did meet thee once with Helena

To do observance to a morn of May,

There will I stay for thee."

"In the wood, a league without the town

To do observance to a morn of May."

Hermia, hearing these words, feels her heart leap with joy. She tries to answer soberly, in the same measure used by her lover; but as her words become impassioned she breaks into rhyme.

My good Lysander!

I swear to thee by Cupid's strongest bow,

By his best arrow with the golden head,

By the simplicity of Venus doves,

By that which knitteth souls and prospers loves,

And by that fire which burn'd the Carthage green,

When the false Trojan under sail was seen;

By all the vows that ever men have broke,

In number more than ever woman spoke,

In that same place thou hast appointed me,

To-morrow truly will I meet with thee.

A scene of homely prose follows. The tradesmen and tinkers of Athens are planning to turn actors and to play "Pyramus and Thisbe" for the Duke's wedding feast. It is full of "local hits," which are not lost upon the audience. In the practical jokes, the melodrama, the ranting bombast, and Bottom's ambition to play "a tyrant's vein," they recognise a satire on the amateur theatricals of the trades-guilds, the clownish horseplay of the "moralities" so-called. These crude plays, once so popular, have become the jest of an audience who pride themselves on a drama of higher ideals and greater art.

A sudden fall of the upper curtain, and the lower stage is concealed, the upper one breaking upon the view of the delighted spectators and announcing Act II of the play. It is a night scene in a wood near Athens; mossy banks and green trees; clouds and twinkling stars in the heavens; forms of fairies sitting about like humming birds, or resting in nodding fern leaves. They sing in quick, short rhymes, suiting the tempo to their actions:--

Woods near Stratford

"Met we on hill, in dale, forest or mead,

By paved fountain or by rushy brook,

Or in the beached margent of the sea,

To dance our ringlets to the whistling wind."

Over hill, over dale,

Thorough flood, thorough fire,

Over park, over pale,

Thorough flood, thorough fire,

I do wander everywhere,

Swifter than the moon's sphere;

And I serve the Fairy Queen,

To dew her orbs upon the green.

The fairy Queen and King appear, engaged in a very human quarrel. Titania, like any mortal woman, is little disposed to yield to the demands of her lord and master one of her cherished treasures. They part in anger, and Oberon summons Puck, the arch mischief maker, and sets on foot the punishment of the rebellious lady. The audience, easy believers in spells, magic, and witchcraft, are in full sympathy with Puck's mission to secure the potion whose magic power will create love or cause infidelity and hatred. Never had poetry been fuller of imagery or sweeter in verification than in the lines spoken by Oberon; nor had Queen Elizabeth ever received a more graceful compliment:--

"Thou rememberest

Since once I sat upon a promontory,

And heard a mermaid on a dolphin's back

Uttering such dulcet and harmonious breath

That the rude sea grew civil at her song,

And certain stars shot madly from their spheres,

To hear the sea maid's music.

That very time I saw, but thou could'st not,

Flying between the cold moon and the earth,

Cupid all arm'd; a certain aim he took

At a fair vestal throned by the West,

And loosed his love-shaft smartly from his bow.

As it should pierce a hundred thousand hearts;

But I might see young Cupid's fiery shaft

Quench'd in the chaste beams of the watery moon,

And the imperial votaress passed on,

In maiden meditation, fancy free.

Yet marked I where the bolt of Cupid fell;

It fell upon a little western flower,

Before milk-white, now purple with love's wound,

And maidens call it love-in-idleness.

Fetch me that flower."

Earl of Leicester receiving Queen Elizabeth at Kenilworth

"And the imperial votaress passed on

In maiden meditation fancy free."

Mark the Queen's flushed cheek and parted lips! The "mermaid on the dolphin's back" is no fancy picture, but an exact description of one of the pageants at the festivities in her honour at Kenilworth. Although twenty years have passed, memory still loves to linger about those days when she visited her favourite, the fascinating Earl of Leicester, on her royal progress, before state policy and private pique had combined to create strife and alienation.

From memory also was the verse-picture painted. The lad of eleven, who had made light of the fifteen miles between Kenilworth and Stratford by tearing across ditch and hedge and meadow, could not easily forget the sights of that memorable day. Little then could he foresee the present hour; but rightly now does he judge that these reminiscences of the olden days will please Her Majesty.

Rightly also does he judge that the ridiculous situations between the lovers will not be displeasing. A Queen whose whole reign has been marked by warfare against the marriage of her courtiers and her clergy, whose own mother's marriage had been so unhappy, will sympathise with Puck when he says of the lovers:--

"Those things do best please me

That fall out preposterously,"

or,

"Lord! What fools these mortals be!"

A mad frolic now begins in fairyland. Puck stirs up all sorts of complications by squeezing the magic flower juice on the wrong eyes with such sad results that Titania falls in love with the weaver, Bottom, with the ass's head on his shoulders; the two friends, Hermia and Helena, rail at each other over the seeming desertion of their lovers. But in the morning, the spell having been removed and each lover restored to his proper relations, the rivals become once more true friends. The fairy King and Queen also have become reconciled, and prepare to celebrate the double wedding of the mortals with sports and revels throughout their fairy kingdom.

Queen Elizabeth in her Later Years

The fifth act restores the lower stage and the palace of Theseus. His wedding festivities have begun. The hard-handed men of Athens perform their crude interlude, made all the more grotesque by the awkwardness of Francis Flute, the bellows-mender. In the character of Thisbe, it is his part to fall upon the sword and die, thus ending the play. Imagine the delight of the courtly auditors when the clumsy man in the part of the disconsolate lady falls, not upon the blade, but upon the scabbard of the unfamiliar weapon!

But laughter and applause are arrested by the appearance of a bright, transparent cloud. It reaches from heaven to earth, and bourne in upon it, with music and with song, are Oberon, Titania, and their elfin train. The cloud parts, and Puck steps forth to speak the epilogue:--

"If we shadows have offended

Think but this, and all is mended.

That you have but slumber'd here

While these visions did appear."

The Christmas play is over, but not over the Christmas fun. Lords and ladies are but human, and have devised a "stately dance," in which they themselves participate until nearly sunrise, the Queen herself joining at times, and never so happy as when assured of her "wondrous majesty and grace."

Did they--did any one--at this Christmas play of three hundred years ago feel the full charm and glory of this immortal creation of the poet? Did its lines ring in their ears the next day, and the next, and the next? Did they foresee how its rhythm would dance down the ages and abide in these present days, and in this present speech of ours?

But this is something that I, your truthful reporter, cannot answer.

A Dance of the Sixteenth Century

"A fortnight hold we this solemnity.

In nightly revels and new jollity."

III.

An Old-Time Christmas Carol.

Sung to the Queen in the Presence at Whitehall MDXCVI.

I sing of a maiden

That is makeless.

King of all kings

To her son she ches.

He came al so still

There his mother was,

As dew in April

That falleth on the grass.

He came al so still

To his mother's bower,

As dew in April

That falleth on the flower.

He came al so still

There his mother lay,

As dew in April

That falleth on the spray.

Mother and maiden

Was never none but she;

Well may such a lady

God's mother be.

Footnote 1: Matchless.
Footnote 2: Chose.

The End

www.ingramcontent.com/pod-product-compliance
Lightning Source LLC
Chambersburg PA
CBHW070513290526
45790CB00003B/1218